HOUSE OF THE RISING SON

Tom Jacobson

I0139732

BROADWAY PLAY PUBLISHING INC
New York
www.broadwayplaypublishing.com
info@broadwayplaypublishing.com

HOUSE OF THE RISING SON
© Copyright 2012 by Tom Jacobson

First printing May 2012
I S B N: 978-0-88145-525-0

Book design: Marie Donovan
Page make-up: Adobe Indesign
Typeface: Palatino
Printed and bound in the U S A

ABOUT THE AUTHOR

Tom Jacobson has had more than 70 productions of
his plays in Los Angeles and around the country,
including SPERM at Circle X Theatre Company,
THE ORANGE GROVE at Playwrights Arena, and
the award-winning BUNBURY, TAINTED BLOOD
and OUROBOROS at The Road Theater Company
(BUNBURY, TAINTED BLOOD, OUROBOROS have
also been published by Broadway Play Publishing Inc).
He has been a co-literary manager of The Theater @
Boston Court, a founding member of Playwrights Ink,
and a board member of Cornerstone Theater Company.
He teaches playwriting and related courses for
U C L A Extension. His most recent productions
were THE FRIENDLY HOUR at The Road (*L A Weekly*
Award for Best Ensemble, and also published by
B P P I), THE TWENTIETH-CENTURY WAY at
The Theater @ Boston Court and the New York
International Fringe Festival (five Ovation Award
nominations, four Los Angeles Drama Critics' Circle
nominations, one GLAAD Award nomination, Fringe
Festival Award for Outstanding Production of a Play),
and MAKING PARADISE: THE WEST HOLLYWOOD
MUSICAL for Cornerstone (Critic's Choice in Back
Stage West). The world premier of THE CHINESE
MASSACRE (ANNOTATED) was recently at Circle X.

HOUSE OF THE RISING SON was first produced by Ensemble Studio Theater-L A (Gates McFadden, Artistic Director; Producing Directors, Laura Flanagan and Sarah Malkin) running from 23 April to 12 June 2011. The cast and creative contributors were:

TRENT ....Paul Witten
FELIX ....Steve Coombs
GARRETT... Patrick John Hurley
BOWEN......................Rod Menzies & Nicholas Hormann

Director...Michael Michetti
Scenic design... Richard Hoover
Lighting design ....Jeremy Pivnick
Original music & sound design............. Bruno Louchouarn
Costume design........................ Christina Haatainen-Jones
Dialect coach... Tray Winters
Stage manager...Nicole Rossi
Production manager ....Rebecca Cohn

CAST OF CHARACTERS

DR. TRENT VARRO, *30s-40s, a parasitologist, also plays*:
   MAUREEN, *organizer of a literary festival*

FELIX MARTIN, *20s-30s, a fundraiser and folklorist, also
plays*:   TOD, *a desperate soul*

GARRETT VARRO, *50s-60s, a restoration architect, also
plays*:   LENDELL, *a psychic tour guide*

BOWEN VARRO, *70s-80s, a poet, also plays*:
   ROBERT, *a gay tour guide*

*The play takes place in various locations in Los Angeles and
New Orleans in the present.*

*Setting: The space should be very simple and mutable,
but evocative of heat and mystery. Locations include an
auditorium, several streets and graveyards, a living room, a
bar, a bedroom, an alley, and a café.*

Note: Doubling is suggested but not required.

ACT ONE

(Lights up on TRENT, *30s-40s, giving a public lecture. He is attractive in an unusual way, not conventionally handsome. He is neatly but casually dressed. His lecture may be accompanied by slides.)*

TRENT: One of the world's most horrifying predators escapes our notice because it's only the size of the head of a pin. The alien that burst out of John Hurt's chest seems positively merciful next to the tiny phorid fly. A common ant going about its daily business of dragging leaves and dead things back to the colony probably doesn't notice the female phorid landing on her back. She may not even feel the fly's ovipositor piercing her head, and the egg extruded into her brain.

FELIX: *(In the front row of the audience.)* Nasty!

TRENT: *(Not hearing* FELIX*)* But slowly, as the baby fly begins to grow, the ant may notice that the larva is beginning to feed. Ants have basic nervous systems, with functions spread throughout the body, not all concentrated in the head, so the ant can continue following scent trails and cleaning herself for a long time.

FELIX: Damn, he's hot.

TRENT: But eventually there's nothing left inside the ant's head but a fat and happy fly larva. At this point the dried-up husk of the head pops off. The ant, poor simple, dedicated worker, continues her tasks—

without a head—until she starves to death because she no longer has a mouth.

FELIX: That is so cool!

TRENT: Parasites are creatures that suck life from other lifeforms from within. The Greek word *parasitos* means "beside food," and originally described ritual food servers—well—waiters: "Hi, my name is Plato and I'll be your parasite this evening." Making their homes beside their food, and often *in* it, parasites are among the most successful living things on the planet. In fact, they constitute about eighty per cent of life on earth.

FELIX: Nice voice. Weird sense of humor.

TRENT: Although they've been inside us for millions of years, only recently did humans start becoming acquainted with our little companions.

FELIX: Step away from the lectern. Let's see the basket.

TRENT: In order to prove that bladder worms inhabiting sheep, pigs and cows were a larval stage of tapeworms that infect predators like dogs, wolves, and humans, in the 1840s Friedrich Kuchenmeister— *(Stepping away from the lectern.)* —Fed bladder worms in a body-temperature soup to a condemned prisoner.

FELIX: Oh, my God. His zipper's down.

TRENT: The prisoner, not knowing what he was eating, asked for seconds. Three days later, after the prisoner's decapitation, Kuchenmeister found small tapeworms in his intestine—

FELIX: And he has no idea.

TRENT: —The prisoner's, that is.

FELIX: That's so embarrassing. *(Shifts in his seat)*

TRENT: In six months we'll open a new exhibition here at the Natural History Museum of Los Angeles County called *Bloodsuckers and Body Snatchers: Parasitism in Nature.* *(Notices* FELIX*)* Mmmm, who's that kid?

FELIX: That's right. It's me.

TRENT: As guest curator, I've gathered specialists from all areas of parasitology to show you their favorite little monsters.

FELIX: Let me taste the wax in your ear.

TRENT: Bladder worms, of course—he's staring, like a stalker.

FELIX: The sweat on your neck.

TRENT: Blood flukes that control the behavior of stickleback fish—did he lick his lips?

FELIX: The musk of your armpits.

TRENT: Two-foot long guinea worms that spool out of your leg when they're laying eggs—straining against his jeans!

FELIX: The reek of your crotch—

TRENT: Sixty-foot tapeworms in whales—barnacles that castrate crabs—is he touching himself?

FELIX: No doubt totally hung.

TRENT: Tapeworms that make beetles bold and foolhardy so they're eaten by rats—he's pinching his nipple!

FELIX: Probably too big for me.

TRENT: Single-celled organisms that make men aggressive and women too friendly—daring me to react!

FELIX: Can I get him in the john?

TRENT: This is the first lecture in a series leading to the opening of the exhibition. Ignore him!

FELIX: Up against the wall—

TRENT: Parasites inhabit an amazing world we never see—our own insides. Don't even look! They're right there all the time, eating, reproducing—a whole world hidden in plain sight. God, they're gonna see my bone! *(Steps quickly behind the lectern)*

(Lighting change as FELIX *joins* TRENT *at the lectern)*

FELIX: Doctor Varro, that was great.

TRENT: Oh...good! Thank you.

FELIX: Very compelling.

TRENT: Not too gross? I get that a lot.

FELIX: I like gross.

TRENT: I kinda noticed that during the lecture.

*(*FELIX *and* TRENT *smile.)*

FELIX: *(Shaking hands)* I'm Felix Martin. I work here at the museum.

TRENT: Doing what?

FELIX: Fundraising—I'm not a scientist. I wonder—

TRENT: Yes?

FELIX: I hesitate to ask—

TRENT: No, that's all right—

FELIX: Because you're not on staff here—but I was wondering if you'd be willing to have dinner—

TRENT: *(Overlapping)* Tonight?

FELIX: —With some of our donors. I've got a couple who are really into parasites.

TRENT: *They* must be interesting.

FELIX: Kinda unusual, but they get it, pretty smart for rich people—

TRENT: You got something against rich people?

FELIX: No! Well, yeah, a little. *(Conspiratorially)* Seems like all they think about is, you know, being rich. But this couple loves all that hidden world stuff you were talking about. I love it, too. Must be cool exploring a whole world like that.

TRENT: Sometimes it's just looking up somebody's butt.

(They both smile.)

FELIX: Oh, by the way—your zipper's down.

(TRENT looks stricken. Lights out on them and up on BOWEN VARRO, 70s-80s, stumbling about drunkenly.)

BOWEN: *(To no one or everyone, in a heavy Southern accent.)* Bienvenue a New Orleans! Ya'll here for the—whatzit—? 'Course you are! Tom—that's what we called him—Tom Williams was my tenant back in the day, that's right.

(GARRETT, 50s-60s, appears.)

GARRETT: Dad, come on! *(Goes to him, gently taking his arm)* Let these people eat their dinner.

BOWEN: They're here for the goddam festival!

GARRETT: *(To the unseen diners)* Sorry, my father's celebrating his tragic longevity—let's go.

BOWEN: I'm in mourning!

GARRETT: Not in Galatoire's, Dad.

BOWEN: This is my son. He tries to keep me out of trouble.

GARRETT: The car's right around the corner.

BOWEN: I had a premonition!

GARRETT: Come have your premonition in the car.

BOWEN: Everything's about to change!

BOWEN:	GARRETT:
Everything!	Everything?

BOWEN: You don't give a shit about our family!

GARRETT: Right, so I guess I should just leave you here to retch on the floor?

BOWEN: *(Swings at* GARRETT, *who easily evades him.)* Some respect, boy!

GARRETT: *(Grabbing him and dragging him out.)* My sincerest apologies to all.

BOWEN: Help, he's taking me to the home!

(Lighting change to FELIX *and* TRENT. *Cricket sounds. It's night and* FELIX *has a flashlight. They're sneaking.)*

TRENT: Don't they have any security? They must've seen us jump the wall.

FELIX: Haven't caught me yet!

TRENT: You do this with every lecturer?

FELIX: If I like the lecture. You afraid of getting in trouble?

TRENT: I'm never afraid of that.

FELIX: *(Pointing)* Look!

TRENT: A pyramid?

FELIX: Rosedale was popular in the twenties, right after Tutankhamen's tomb was excavated, so lots of mausoleums were built in Egyptian style. I'm terrible on history, but I know graveyards. Oh, and this is pretty cool. *(Points at the ground.)*

TRENT: *(Peering)* Hattie McDaniel? Who was she?

FELIX: You're kidding, you're from New Orleans and you don't know Hattie McDaniel? She played Mammy in *Gone with the Wind.*

TRENT: Who remembers actors' names?

FELIX: You believe in ghosts?

TRENT: I'm a biologist.

FELIX: I don't know if I believe in 'em either—

TRENT: *(Overlapping)* I *don't* believe—

FELIX: But I love ghost stories. I got an M A in folklore at U C L A, which as you can imagine led me directly to fundraising 'cause A) you can't do shit with an M A in folklore and B) I'll be damned if I go through seven years of a PhD just so I can teach.

TRENT: So you gave it up?

FELIX: Not at all—I'm almost done writing a book, well not so much writing as collecting ghost stories from all over—wanna hear one?

TRENT: In a graveyard at night with a cute but strange guy I just met?

FELIX: Worse yet, a sell-out. A *fundraiser.*

TRENT: I'm a sell-out as well. I write for the lay reader rather than scientific journals.

FELIX: I know. I read both your books.

TRENT: Really? Both?

FELIX: You're different from other scientists. You like the stories best, too.

TRENT: All right. Tell me the ghost story.

FELIX: When I was in college I met this girl who saw auras and spoke in tongues and stuff like that. She also told me she saw faces.

TRENT: What kind of faces?

FELIX: Faces on faces. From past lives. Once she was with a girlfriend of hers and saw this horrible evil hairy ugly face on the friend's face. So she said something, like, I dunno, "excuse me, but you've got a horrible evil hairy ugly face on." And suddenly the face kinda detached itself from the friend and came at her, and she felt this wave of horror and hatred and disgust. Isn't that creepy?

TRENT: But not really a ghost story exactly.

FELIX: You're right. See—I'm a terrible folklorist.

(A strange animal wails in the near distance.)

FELIX: Oh my God! It's a *chupacabra*! *(Runs off with his flashlight)*

TRENT: A what? Felix! Don't—! *(Giggles as he disappears after* FELIX.) What the hell are you looking for?

(Lighting change. BOWEN *and* GARRETT *are in a car, with* GARRETT *driving.)*

BOWEN: Why'd you let him go to Los Angeles?

GARRETT: That your premonition?

BOWEN: Stupid little faggot.

GARRETT: Don't talk like that.

BOWEN: No one can hear me but you.

GARRETT: I don't wanna hear that kinda talk about Trent.

BOWEN: Faggotpansycocksuckerpantywaistqueer.

*(*GARRETT *rolls his eyes as the lights change to* FELIX *and* TRENT. *It's still night and they're still outdoors. Cricket and other insect sounds.)*

FELIX: Hollywood Forever is kinda touristy as you might expect. So it's my *second* favorite graveyard. Cecil B DeMille is over there—that big monument, and Douglas Fairbanks—

TRENT: Please tell me you've never seen a ghost.

FELIX: Gay people have a shamanistic role in our society, and if anybody should see ghosts, it should be us.

TRENT: So you're a shaman?

FELIX: I studied up, did spiritual exercises, went to psychics, a seance, but I guess I'm not attuned.

TRENT: Thank God.

FELIX: But I do like knowing shit nobody else knows. Not in a braggy way, just—

TRENT: Knowledge for its own sake.

FELIX: Like science.

(They smile.)

TRENT: Nobody in Minnesota sees ghosts. Very stolid population.

FELIX: Minnesota? I thought you were from New Orleans.

TRENT: High school in New Orleans—we moved there—my family—originally from Minnesota—

FELIX: I wondered why no accent.

TRENT: Ever been to New Orleans? Lotta ghosts there— they say.

FELIX: I bet! I've never been.

TRENT: You'd fit right in.

FELIX: And I always wanted to—but isn't it still fucked up from the hurricane and the oil spill?

TRENT: In recovery. Could you take tomorrow off?

FELIX: To go to New Orleans?

TRENT: For a long weekend.

FELIX: I got a couple of appointments….

TRENT: Be sick.

FELIX: I met you all of two hours ago—

TRENT: We've shared two cemeteries. You could bone up on shamanism.

FELIX: I dunno.

TRENT: I'm going back anyway. I have a series of parasite lectures at Tulane, which is an excuse to spend some time with my family.

FELIX: You want me to meet your parents?

TRENT: *(Uncomfortable)* Well, yeah, my parents—

TRENT:	FELIX:
—Plus it's the Tennessee Williams Literary Festival— lots of stories for you—	Oh, God. What's wrong with them?

FELIX: I barely know you—we haven't even—

TRENT: Eaten! I'm starving and you're dragging me to graveyards. *(Pulls out a cell phone, dials.)*

FELIX: There's a twenty-four hour—

TRENT: *(Into the phone)* Hey.

FELIX: Who are you—?

TRENT: What are you doing still up? *(Listens)* Just knock him on the head and hope he lands in bed. Listen, is it okay if I bring a friend for the weekend? *(Listens)* Yes. Exactly. That all right? You okay with that? *(Listens)* No, I'll get a—*we'll* get a cab. Go give grandpa some aspirin and vitamin C. Good-night.

FELIX: I can't really afford—I mean, on short notice tickets will be—

TRENT: Don't worry, I'm buying.

FELIX: No way.

TRENT: I'm the one dragging you home to meet the family—I should pay.

FELIX: No, I should.

TRENT: You will.

FELIX: Dude, I can't just drop everything—

TRENT: You go cemetery hopping all night but can't hop on a plane? Afraid of getting in trouble?

(They stare at each other. FELIX looks away.)

FELIX: *(Spying something on the ground)* There it is! *(He pulls a paper and crayon from his pocket, drops to the ground, and makes a rubbing of a stone.)*

TRENT: Now we can add vandalism to trespassing.

(Lighting change to GARRETT and BOWEN at home. GARRETT brings BOWEN some pills and water.)

GARRETT: He's bringing someone.

BOWEN: Someone who can help pass on the family name?

GARRETT: Don't get too optimistic.

BOWEN: Optimistic? I told you I had a premonition. Here it is coming true.

GARRETT: When they get here, tone it down, okay?

BOWEN: Tone what down?

GARRETT: The talk, you know. It puts people off, first impressions—

BOWEN: Goddam, I'm sick of this crap!

GARRETT: That's what I mean—

BOWEN: Every day, same piddly-ass—

GARRETT: Don't make me lock you in your room.

BOWEN: Every goddam day for my whole life, you realize?

GARRETT: When some people get drunk, they get philosophical. You just get stupid.

BOWEN: How many years I been doing this? I gotta eat—three times a day—

GARRETT: At least.

BOWEN: Shit once a day—

GARRETT & BOWEN: *(Simultaneously)* —If I'm/you're lucky—

BOWEN: Brush my teeth, take a shower, have something to drink—!

GARRETT: Don't forget that—

BOWEN: Every damn day! I'm bored with it. Aren't you? It just goes on and on into endless tedium. And *breathing!* Think how often we have to do that! How many breaths do I have to draw a day, each one just like the last?

GARRETT: Just help me get through this with Trent, then you can boycott breathing. I need you to behave yourself.

(BOWEN *looks annoyed and closes his eyes. Lights up on* TRENT *and* FELIX *as well. They are in another cemetery,* FELIX *searching the ground with the flashlight. An even greater variety of insect sounds.)*

FELIX: So you still live with your parents?

TRENT: Sort of, off and on.

FELIX: At your age?

TRENT: At their age, sometimes they need help.

FELIX: You're the good son.

(TRENT *laughs.)*

FELIX: So you're out to them?

TRENT: Oh, yes, in fact—

FELIX: My mom and I don't speak.

TRENT: I'm sorry. Although sometimes I wish my folks didn't speak. They find me—

FELIX: Rebellious?

TRENT: They say I provoke people.

(FELIX *and* TRENT *stare at each other.* FELIX *looks away.)*

FELIX: *(Spies something on the ground)* Finally! *(Kneels to make another rubbing.)*

TRENT: Breaking into three graveyards in one night, just to get—

FELIX: Graveyards freak you out?

TRENT: I'm from New Orleans—I live in a graveyard. But there's something very *Harold and Maude* about this.

(BOWEN *has gotten very still. Even his breathing seems to have stopped.* GARRETT *watches him with concern.)*

FELIX: *(Rubbing)* You do know movies! Forest Lawn is the most famous L A cemetery of all. You ever see *The Loved One*?

TRENT: Don't think so.

GARRETT: *(Quietly)* Bowen.

FELIX: Very dark comedy based on a Evelyn Waugh novel making fun of California and the death industry. It was all about Forest Lawn.

(FELIX *holds up the rubbing paper, which clearly says* "TRENT AND FELIX". TRENT *smiles and takes the paper.)*

GARRETT: *(Louder)* Bowen?

BOWEN: *(Starting awake)* What, goddammit?

TRENT: Does this mean you'll fly home with me?

FELIX: Not ready to take that step.

GARRETT: Don't stop breathing yet.

FELIX: *(Overlapping)* Yet.

BOWEN: Don't lock me in my goddamn room.

GARRETT: Then watch your vocabulary.

FELIX: I think Bette Davis is here somewhere.

(GARRETT *walks away from* BOWEN *into darkness as he speaks. At the same time,* FELIX *briefly shines the flashlight onto* GARRETT. *The insect sounds cease instantly.*)

GARRETT: I won't warn you again.

(Lights out on GARRETT *and* BOWEN *completely.)*

FELIX: *(Turning to run)* Okay, let's go.

TRENT: *(Stopping him)* Why?

FELIX: That guy saw us. You heard him.

TRENT: What guy? There's nobody here.

FELIX: He walked right into my light. He said he's not warning us again. C'mon!

TRENT: *(Grabbing the light, shining it about)* There's nobody there. We're all alone in the middle of Forest Lawn in the middle of the night.

FELIX: You didn't see him?

TRENT: *(Playing the light around)* Not then, not now.

(The insect sounds return.)

FELIX: He was *right there!* How could you not see him?

TRENT: What'd he look like? Was he wearing a shroud?

FELIX: He just looked like…a guy. Fifty, sixty something. Nondescript, wearing khakis, kinda cute even, for a guy that age—

TRENT: Maybe you just saw your first ghost.

FELIX: In khakis?

TRENT: From Dead Gap.

FELIX: I wish! Like I said—I got no abilities. Oh my God—an open grave?

TRENT: Dare you.

FELIX: Dare me what?

TRENT: Pussy. Take that step.

FELIX: What if that guy's still here?

TRENT: Maybe it's his grave. C'mon!

(Lighting change as FELIX *and* TRENT *jump into an open grave. They stand there nervously.)*

FELIX: Okay, this is way eerie. *(Measuring above his head.)* It's exactly six feet deep.

TRENT: You scared?

FELIX: No! Yes! *(Grabs* TRENT *for comfort)* I might throw up.

TRENT: Your heart's beating really fast.

FELIX: You're not even a little bit scared?

TRENT: Okay, I've got tears in my eyes—how's that?

FELIX: *(Turning toward* TRENT*)* Tears are good. Anything else?

TRENT: Yeah.

*(*TRENT *kisses* FELIX *hard. They grope each other frantically.)*

FELIX: *(As they make out)* This is somebody's grave! We're like your parasites.

TRENT: How?

FELIX: Copulating like little hookworms in an intestine.

TRENT: Surrounded by bodies upon bodies upon bodies.

FELIX: All filled with bacteria and amoebas—

(The insect sounds gradually increase.)

TRENT: *(As they sink to the bottom of the grave)* All munching away—

FELIX: Inside the bodies—

TRENT/FELIX:
Inside *your/my* body—living off you/me.

TRENT: You *have* to come to New Orleans!

(TRENT *rims* FELIX.)

FELIX: *(Almost gasping)* All right—I'm coming!

(The insect sounds reach a climax and the lights go out on TRENT and FELIX. Lights up on BOWEN and GARRETT. GARRETT sniffs BOWEN's breath.)

BOWEN: Sober as a judge.

GARRETT: Forgive me for checking.

BOWEN: I do not take this lightly.

GARRETT: I know.

BOWEN: Nothing could be more important to this family.

GARRETT: You hardly have to inculcate *me*.

BOWEN: You're too damn lenient, permissive. He manipulates you.

GARRETT: He's not a kid. I can't control him.

BOWEN: Never could.

(Sound of a key in a door. GARRETT and BOWEN visibly stiffen. TRENT walks in with luggage and FELIX. When FELIX sees GARRETT, he gasps and drops his luggage. GARRETT and BOWEN just stare at FELIX.)

TRENT: Felix, this is my father, Garrett Varro—

(Nobody says anything.)

TRENT: —And my grandfather, Bowen Varro.

(Still everyone remains frozen.)

TRENT: How about a little southern hospitality, *y'all*?

FELIX: Nice to meet you.

BOWEN: Garrett—

GARRETT: Dad, I won't warn you again.

FELIX: Shit!

BOWEN: Don't *Dad* me! *(He starts to leave.)*

TRENT: Grandpa!

BOWEN: *(Wheeling on* TRENT*)* Mendacity!

TRENT: Oh, please! No more festival events for you!

BOWEN: *(To* GARRETT*)* He's creating a situation—!

GARRETT: Hush, Dad!

*(*GARRETT *reaches for* FELIX's *hand.* FELIX *flinches, but shakes it.)*

GARRETT: Nice to meet you, Felix. Dad, you be nice.

FELIX: *(Almost unable to breathe)* H—h—hello.

TRENT: Grandpa?

BOWEN: *(With an audible sigh.)* Greetings, young man. We've heard *so little* about you.

TRENT: Felix works at the Natural History Museum in L A. He's never been to New Orleans. He likes ghost stories.

BOWEN: Ghost stories?

FELIX: Yes…ghosts— *(Glances at* GARRETT*)* I like them.

BOWEN: Welcome to America's most haunted city. Is Trent taking you on one of the ghost tours?

GARRETT:	BOWEN:
Complete waste of money.	Macabre enough right here.

BOWEN: *(To* TRENT, *with an edge)* He likes ghosts. Hideous, the luggage.

(As GARRETT *picks up* FELIX's *dropped luggage.)*

BOWEN: We had Celeste freshen up my grandson's old room—

FELIX: *(Reaching for the luggage)* Oh, no, I can—

GARRETT: You're the guest. Relax.

GARRETT:	BOWEN:
I'm sure someone here	Our honored guest.
knows how to fix you a	
drink.	

FELIX: That's okay, I don't—

BOWEN: Don't *drink*? This is New Orleans, boy!

FELIX: I just got here—

GARRETT:	BOWEN:
(Reaching for FELIX's	To toast your arrival.
backpack) I can take that, too	We're obligated.

FELIX: *(Flinching again)* Really, I—thanks—yeah, a drink
would be great. I'll keep this.

(GARRETT leaves with the luggage but not the backpack.
TRENT *makes drinks.)*

TRENT: How about a Sazerac?

BOWEN: For me, too. Sit down, young man, and I'll
tell you a good Southern ghost story. About this very
house, once a well-known brothel—

TRENT: Not true.

BOWEN:	FELIX:
It's true to me. Felix—sit!	I'm sorry—I'm just a
Don't stand there so	little—
awkwardly.	

FELIX: *(Fumbling for a pen and pad)* Do you mind if I—?

BOWEN: Not at all, this is highly quotable. When I
was much younger, much, much younger, back when
Louisiana still belonged to France—just kidding—

FELIX: How long have you lived in New Orleans?

BOWEN: All my live-long days. I *earned* this accent.

(FELIX *looks quizzically at* TRENT, *who ignores him while fixing drinks.*)

BOWEN: Back in the days of daguerreotypes—

TRENT: Gramps—

BOWEN: *Mon cher petit-fils* loathes exaggeration. Pure horseshit straight from the gelding, however—

TRENT: We don't have to stay here, you know—

BOWEN: Years ago—*years*—I was sitting here in front of this very window with my father when a family friend took a picture. Casual little candid shot. None of us thought about it much, didn't even bother to get the film developed for a month. When we did, call it distortion, call it reflection of the flash, but there was a deformed, demonic face in the window— *(Stands and gestures head high)* —Right about there. Head high. Glowing. And glowing just the same, on my father's shoulder— *(Puts his hand on* FELIX'*s shoulder)* —Was resting a hand. None of us woulda thought a thing about it, like I said, just a bad flash photo, except that three days after the picture was taken, my father died.

FELIX: Chills! Excellent! Do you have it?

BOWEN: The photograph? Oh, somewheres…I ain't the most organized—

GARRETT: *(Entering)* It's in the archive by date, nineteen—

BOWEN: Enough, *son*! My age is mythic, not specific. Hideous here maintains the family history, all the photographs and records, conserved 'em after Katrina, skills from his indentured servitude at Taliesin West—

FELIX:	TRENT:
Were—were you a Taliesin	Grandpa—!
Fellow?	

GARRETT: You've been to Taliesin?

FELIX: I guy I dated was a Fellow there, briefly. When were you there?

GARRETT: Too long ago to remember.

FELIX: Did you work with the archivist?

BOWEN: That old queen.

GARRETT: *(A warning)* Dad—

(BOWEN shoves his fist in his mouth.)

TRENT: I didn't bring Felix here for a festival of homophobia. There's always Somat House—

GARRETT: Trent, you know how he is—

TRENT: Which is why I've been in L A for the last year! Our politics don't mix.

FELIX: It's okay—

TRENT: It is *not* okay. If I bring home someone I'm fucking—

| FELIX: | GARRETT: |
| Trent, damn! | Don't get him going— |

BOWEN: Oh, so you fuck him? He takes it up the ass?

TRENT: He takes my tongue up his ass.

BOWEN: How's that taste? *(To FELIX)* You keep yourself clean, boy?

(FELIX is mortified and GARRETT simply leaves the room.)

TRENT: He's dirty, and I like him that way.

FELIX: Oh, my God—

BOWEN: He shit in your mouth? *(To FELIX)* You shit in his little faggot mouth?

(Instant lighting change and BOWEN disappears in darkness. FELIX is shaken.)

TRENT: Sorry about that.

FELIX: I am so freaked out right now.

TRENT: *Grand-pere's* always been kinda—

FELIX: No—not just your grandfather—your father is the guy—

TRENT: What guy?

FELIX: Garrett—your dad—is the guy I saw at Forest Lawn.

TRENT: The ghost?

FELIX: Or whatever. Spitting image. Even the voice is the same: "I won't warn you again." Exactly what he said in the graveyard.

TRENT: Perhaps you're a little too immersed in your book research. Forget about ghosts—I'm sorry they were so harsh on you. Especially Grandpa.

FELIX: How's your mother put up with that?

TRENT: She's dead.

FELIX: Your grandmother?

TRENT: Dead, too.

FELIX: You bait him.

TRENT: He rises to it.

FELIX: He likes it! Old people aren't supposed to talk like that! Why didn't you warn me?

TRENT: Some things have to be seen to be believed. Would you have come?

FELIX: Your dad's polite, but he doesn't like me, either. How'd you turn out so normal growing up with those homophobes?

TRENT: Made my politics pretty rad for a while.

(FELIX *snickers.*)

TRENT: What?

FELIX: Rad. That's cute.

TRENT: Ageist.

FELIX: Your politics ever creep into your lectures?

TRENT: Nope. Entirely separate. I've organized my share of queer demonstrations, but there's scant research on the sexual orientation of parasites.

FELIX: (Gesturing for separation) Your work—and your life.

TRENT: Exactly. The only gay scientists are botanists.

FELIX: So much for that. I know how scientists are, but how can you hide—?

TRENT:	FELIX:
Gimme a break.	Professional and personal integrity—

TRENT: Everybody my generation grew up with intolerant colleagues and homophobic relatives.

FELIX: Ageist.

TRENT: And they're pissed I'm not doing things their way.

FELIX: Clearly. You're a much more understanding son than they deserve.

TRENT: Bowen's heart's in the right place.

FELIX: But it's a *spleen.*

TRENT: He's on a lot of drugs.

FELIX: At his age?

TRENT: Not fun drugs. Chemotherapy.

FELIX: Oh. What kind?

TRENT: Prostate.

FELIX: I'm sorry.

TRENT: It's no excuse, but the hormone therapy gives him mood swings. This was happy.

FELIX: Damn! But he *was* happy fighting with you. And you ate it up. Amazing!

(Doorbell rings. TRENT goes to answer it.)

TRENT: I think he actually likes you. This is only one of his personalities.

FELIX: Wait, I don't get it—you said your family's from Minnesota but he said he's from here.

TRENT: My mother's family—

FELIX: Yeah, but—no—huh?

(TRENT opens the door, revealing LENDELL, played by the same actor as GARRETT. He's dressed like a middle-aged Goth or 19th-century undertaker.)

LENDELL: *(Sepulchral)* Pardon me, is this the Varro household?

TRENT: Yes.

LENDELL: May I speak to Garrett Varro, please? My name is Lendell Blosser, and I wanted to ask him about including this house in our Ghosts of New Orleans tour.

TRENT: Garrett went out, but I don't think we'd want—

LENDELL: It is haunted, isn't it? I've heard rumors for years.

TRENT: That's just—

LENDELL: Yes—yes! I'm sensing a presence—!

(Instant lighting change and TRENT and LENDELL disappear. BOWEN reappears near FELIX.)

BOWEN: Well, ain't you the turd that won't flush?

FELIX: I'm sorry, I was just—

BOWEN: Sit down. I've been wanting to talk to you without Trent around to fuck things up.

FELIX: You sure?

BOWEN: This insipid bitch from the festival is coming over to get some snapshots, but till she does—

FELIX: Why is she a bitch?

BOWEN: She's got this godawful laugh. I hate women's voices, so high and irritating.

FELIX: Misogynist, too—

BOWEN: What?

FELIX: Nothing.

BOWEN: What's it you like about Trent? He's a squirrelly kid.

FELIX: Hardly a kid. He's at least ten, fifteen years older than me.

BOWEN: And you like that?

FELIX: A) guys my age aren't all that smart, usually, at least not in L A, and B) not about things I care about.

BOWEN: Like parasites?

FELIX: More than eighty percent of the world's—

BOWEN: Like you gave a shit about that before yesterday.

BOWEN:	FELIX:
There's more to Trent than entertainingly gruesome statistics.	I've done my own research online— Did he *tell* you about his work on elephantiasis in Africa?

FELIX: That the disease that makes your balls swell up like basketballs?

BOWEN: Technically, it's your scrotum, not your balls, but yes. Trent was one of the researchers who discovered the worms that cause it can be paralyzed with some cheap drug. And he persuaded the pharmaceutical company to donate enough to cure everybody that has it.

FELIX: That is so totally cool! Why doesn't he mention that in his books?

BOWEN: He prefers to be a naughty boy.

FELIX: Yeah, but for all his—I dunno—expertise and his bad boy attitude, he's still kinda like a kid, kinda naïve, kinda vulnerable.

BOWEN: Vulnerable?

FELIX: In his challenges, you gotta see that, when he— speaks like that to you—he's compensating, insecure, vulnerable.

BOWEN: And you like *that*?

FELIX: I guess I shouldn't expect you to see it—but I think he wants your approval—

BOWEN: You saying I'm not sensitive?

FELIX: Well—

BOWEN: I'm damn sensitive! You like poetry?

FELIX: I guess. Some.

BOWEN: Emily Dickinson? Candy-ass Robert Frost? *Rod McKuen?*

FELIX: Rimbaud. Baudelaire.

BOWEN: *(Finding some paper)* Any *living* poets?

FELIX: Aren't all poets dead?

BOWEN: This was written by a young man who lives in the attic.

(BOWEN *hands it to* FELIX, *who reads silently.)*

FELIX: Um…this is about shit.

BOWEN: That's right. A fundamental function. He's got the common touch.

FELIX: This is a shit poem.

BOWEN: It's full of practical advice.

FELIX: *(Reading)* "Never wash your anus with soap."

BOWEN: It's a delicate mucus membrane. Meant to be clean, but not sterile. You wouldn't put soap in your eye, would you?

FELIX: *(Reading)* "Get your caca consolidated."

BOWEN: That's my favorite line. Stuttering alliteration.

FELIX: It's horrible.

(Doorbell rings. BOWEN moves to answer it.)

BOWEN: It's contemporary. Break out of the nineteenth century, boy. Young people are so goddam prissy these days!

(BOWEN lets MAUREEN into the room. She is in a nice suit and played by TRENT.)

MAUREEN: *(Southern accent)* Mister Varro, thanks so much for seeing me. *(Seeing FELIX)* Oh, I'm so sorry— you have company! I can come back another time.

BOWEN: It's fine, Maureen, I got the pictures handy.

FELIX: Hi, I'm Felix.

BOWEN: Felix was born during Mister Reagan's presidency.

FELIX: I'm a friend of Trent.

MAUREEN: Oh, Trent makes his daddy and grand-daddy so proud. All that incomprehensible but important work he does with worms and other squishy things. *(Cheerfully)* Disgusting! *(Shaking hands)* I'm Maureen. I don't know if Mister Varro's told you, but I help put together our little Williams Festival, and he's got the perfect pictures for our photomontage slide presentation on the final night. *(To BOWEN)* It's so kind of you to let such precious things out of your sight for even a minute. *(Looking at a picture)* Oh, this is you, isn't it? *With* Tennessee, how exciting! And how young! *(Dabs eyes)* Oh, I must apologize! I've been running this festival too long—every little thing connected to Tennessee just makes me puddle up! Is he giving you an award?

BOWEN: Some literary thing.

MAUREEN: Don't be so modest! Poet laureate of the state of Louisiana. You and Tenn look so happy.

BOWEN: Gloating toad-frogs of fame.

(MAUREEN laughs in an irritating way. BOWEN reacts.)

FELIX: You're the young man in the attic.

MAUREEN: Well, of course! That was the title of his first collection. *(Looking at another picture)* Is this the house you rented Tenn in nineteen—?

BOWEN: *(Quickly)* Yes.

MAUREEN: *(To FELIX)* The Varros owned half the Quarter at one time. Very old New Orleans family. Just couldn't have the Festival without 'em! *(Laughs her irritating laugh.)*

(Instant lighting change puts MAUREEN and FELIX in the dark as BOWEN is isolated in light with GARRETT.)

BOWEN: Mendacity!

GARRETT: I'm not apologizing—

BOWEN: Your *son* is a deceiving little cocksucker. Bringing that boy into this house under these circumstances—

GARRETT: Trent has to do things his own way.

BOWEN: But he can't force us to accept, condone, abet and *facilitate*—

GARRETT: Just go along with him for now. He'll come around. Has to.

BOWEN: I'm too old for this shit. You wanna dissemble like that you go ahead.

GARRETT: I think I have to.

BOWEN: No, we don't. We should—*you should*—just tell him the way things are and be done with it.

GARRETT: I'll take care of it.

BOWEN: It's your job—don't involve me. This family is your responsibility, no longer my concern.

GARRETT: Mendacity!

BOWEN: Very well, it's my concern, but ain't much I can do at this point. Used to be what I said went, but no more. We had some standards, some traditions, ways of doing things—

GARRETT: And I'm doing the same things—you know I am, hard as it is—

BOWEN: Just keep this family going, that's all I'm asking. I told you I had a premonition.

GARRETT: The world's not the same—we can't always do things the same way—

BOWEN: Oh, so we should adapt—?

GARRETT: That's right.

BOWEN: Like one of Trent's slimy little tapeworms. I'm a man, not a goddam invertebrate!

GARRETT: Then act like a man and help with this. Or at least don't make it harder than it is.

BOWEN: I'm done. I quit. I haven't the energy. I'm just gonna sit here like a turtle in my shell.

GARRETT: That will do.

(*As* GARRETT *and* BOWEN *glare at each other,* TRENT *and* FELIX *appear, isolated in another pool of light.*)

FELIX: I don't get it.

TRENT: What's to get?

FELIX: I'm sure you mean well and maybe you're trying to spare me from something—more homophobic abuse no doubt—

TRENT: I want you to get to know them slowly. They're kind of overwhelming—

FELIX: You coulda told me more in advance—

TRENT: Like what?

FELIX: Like your grandfather's some kinda famous poet.

TRENT: Not any more. He's too focused on the parts of his body that don't work.

FELIX: And you're totally rich and living off your family.

(TRENT *doesn't speak.*)

BOWEN: Time for me to leave.

GARRETT: Leave?

BOWEN: This earthly plane.

FELIX:	GARRETT:
Aren't you?	Don't talk like that.

TRENT:	BOWEN:
Not totally.	I'm ready even if you're not.

FELIX:	GARRETT:
Only own half the French Quarter.	Don't make me wish I was ready.

TRENT: I dunno. Dad handles all that.

(BOWEN *glares at* GARRETT, *then begins to sing.*)

FELIX: Maybe you can be casual about it, but it's all new to me—I'm no trust fund baby—is that why you put up with all that crap? To get your money?

BOWEN:	FELIX:
Swing low, sweet chariot	I work with rich people all
Comin' for to carry me	day, and I hate to think of
home!	you like that—a slave to
	your inheritance—

(Instant lighting change puts FELIX *in the dark and* TRENT *in the same space as* GARRETT *and* BOWEN.*)*

TRENT, GARRETT & BOWEN: *(Singing in harmony)*
Swing low, sweet chariot
Comin' for to carry me home!

TRENT: Not yet, Grandpa. You've got business to attend to.

GARRETT & BOWEN: What?

TRENT: Felix.

BOWEN: Felix ain't the issue.

TRENT: Yes, he is. Whether you acknowledge it or not.

BOWEN: Lying is the issue.

TRENT: You lie all the time.

BOWEN: Not this way. What the hell do you think you're doing?

TRENT: Patience, Grandpa, patience.

*(*BOWEN *glares.)*

TRENT: Do you like him?

BOWEN: Goddammit, Trent! He's a little prissy pants.

TRENT: He's idealistic. I don't expect you to remember that far back. *(To* GARRETT*)* I was asking *you.*

GARRETT: I've hardly spent five minutes with him.

TRENT: Would you, please?

GARRETT: I don't know any ghost stories.

BOWEN: Yes, you do.

TRENT: The ghost stories are a little silly, but he's got a real responsible job—

BOWEN: Bilking money outta people—

TRENT: For a natural history museum—

BOWEN: For a bunch of stuffed giraffes and monkeys—

GARRETT: A dead zoo.

BOWEN: What kind of accomplishment is that? Talk about a parasite!

TRENT: He hates it, okay? Wealth gives him the willies 'cause his mom had to sell Mary Kay to put him through college. *We* give him the willies. Sometimes we give *me* the willies!

GARRETT: Let's not get off track. Whether we acknowledge it or not, we're talking about our family's future here, right?

BOWEN: We are indeed.

TRENT: Okay, yeah, so?

GARRETT: You have a responsibility—

TRENT: I have a responsibility to myself.

BOWEN: Self, self, self! The mantra of youth!

GARRETT: You have to think about us as well.

TRENT: I am. Just have coffee with him. *(Shows paper rubbing of* "TRENT AND FELIX"*)* He gave me this.

BOWEN: Childish.

GARRETT: You have before you a choice.

BOWEN: And so do we. Do not make a foolish one.

(Instant lighting change puts BOWEN *and* TRENT *in darkness and isolates* GARRETT *and* FELIX *sitting at a small café table with two cups of coffee and some beignets.)*

FELIX: Not much of a choice.

GARRETT: *(Fairly uptight)* People come here just for
coffee and beignets, so that's all they sell.

FELIX: *(Eating)* Good, though.

GARRETT: Are you from Los Angeles originally?

FELIX: The Valley.

GARRETT: Do you like it?

FELIX: It's cool.

GARRETT: Miserably designed. L A, not the Valley.
Well, the Valley, too.

FELIX: L A's not designed at all, just sort of vomited all
over.

GARRETT: Exactly.

FELIX: But I love the architecture.

GARRETT: The architecture? In L A?

FELIX: It's so damn goofy! So—I dunno—flawed.

GARRETT: No city has destroyed more of its
architectural heritage—no sense of tradition—tore
down the Neutra house—

FELIX: That was Palm Springs.

GARRETT: Practically L A. Unacceptable!

FELIX: I agree. But once I was on top of the L A County
Museum of Art—

GARRETT: That's not even architecture!

FELIX: And I looked around the city—panoramic
view—and I could see Park LaBrea, which is basically
projects for yuppies, the blue whale—the Pacific
Design Center, the *Diehard* building out at Fox, the
Hollywood sign, and the bizarre Pavilion for Japanese
Art—

GARRETT:	FELIX:
Bruce Goff was the only	The Broad Contemporary

visionary architect that   Art Museum—
worked on that place—
The Broad? A box with a   —The Resnick Pavilion—
buzz-cut—!   and it was all so frail, so
                               silly, so *human*, that I had
                               to love it. Not crystallized
                               like other cities—New
                               York, Chicago, San
                               Francisco, New Orleans—

GARRETT: It has no history to speak of.

FELIX: It's not trapped by its history.

GARRETT: Nothing to build on.

FELIX: L A hasn't found itself yet. My heart went out to
it.

GARRETT: You're attracted to vulnerability.

FELIX: I guess.

GARRETT: But Trent—

FELIX: Been talking to your dad?

GARRETT: You told him that's what you liked about
Trent.

FELIX: I like flaws.

GARRETT: Very worldly—for such a young man.

FELIX: I'm too young for Trent? That your issue?

GARRETT: Oh, no, not at all.

FELIX: Look, I'm sure you—and especially your
father—have some very outdated notions of what gay
people—gay men—are like.

GARRETT: Just because we live in New Orleans
doesn't mean we're— *(Mimes playing the theme from*
Deliverance *on a banjo.)* Ding de ding ding ding ding
ding ding ding—

FELIX: We're not all running down the street with our dick out all the time.

(GARRETT *chokes on his coffee.*)

FELIX: Sorry. That was coarse, but you know what I mean—

GARRETT: No—just—the image—

FELIX: These days, my mom and I are—well—*estranged*—is the nice way to put it. She's religious. And I never knew my dad.

GARRETT: Sorry to hear it.

FELIX: So basically I have no family and I'm looking for one. Trent could be—I mean I have no idea—we just met—but I'm intrigued by the possibility—and my intention, whether it's Trent or someone else—is to be with him. Just him. I had my wild time when I was younger, but A) I kinda got it out of my system and B) I don't want a relationship like my parents apparently had—my mother told me she once broke a full-length mirror over my father's head—I want something more—I dunno—*reliable*. Know what I mean?

GARRETT: You have great expectations.

FELIX: Unrealistic, you mean.

GARRETT: Your generation is so…rigid.

FELIX: We know what we want.

GARRETT: I know how men are. Not just homosexuals. I don't think there's much of a difference. Men. Fidelity. I'm skeptical. And *two* men—*well*—

FELIX: *That's* a generational attitude. The world has changed. But I understand. I don't expect you to—

GARRETT: How's your coffee?

FELIX: Excellent.

GARRETT: Chicory. *(Blows powdered sugar from the beignet onto* FELIX.*)*

FELIX: Hey!

GARRETT: Tradition. You wanna hear a ghost story?

FELIX: Of course! *(Pulling out his pad)* First person?

GARRETT: From when I was a kid.

FELIX: Great. And I've got one for you, too, sort of. Remind me.

GARRETT: I was staying with my grandmother in Yazoo City, Mississippi. I woke up in the middle of the night and saw an old man with long white hair sitting on the floor at the foot of the bed, bowing to me. I hid under the covers, called to my grandmother, and she told me to go back to sleep. Years later, I was looking at some old family pictures—nineteenth century, very formal—and there he was. My grandmother told me he was my great great grandfather, who was part Indian, uh, Native American. Cherokee or Choctaw, she thought. Not that I believe in ghosts or anything.

FELIX: Did she believe you?

GARRETT: I never told her. You don't have to tell people everything.

FELIX: Thanks for telling me. Payback: I think I saw a ghost once.

GARRETT: Where?

FELIX: In L A. In a cemetery the night I met Trent. You'll never guess what he looked like.

*(*FELIX *blows powdered sugar on* GARRETT. *Lighting change.* TRENT *is delivering his first lecture at Tulane.)*

TRENT: The cleverest parasites are masters of manipulation that put Machiavelli to shame. The barnacle *Sacculina* weaves its roots throughout the

body of a crab, sucking life from its blood, preventing
the crab from going about its normal business
of finding a mate and laying eggs. No energy is
devoted to activities other than those that serve the
parasite. *Sacculina*, in effect, chemically castrates the
crab, preventing the female from laying eggs, and
effeminizing the male. But both male and female crabs
retain a maternal instinct, and when the barnacle eggs
appear—where the crab's eggs would normally grow
on its abdomen—the crab cleans them and cares for
them as if they are her own—or his own. The parasite
turns its host into a surrogate parent, an arthropod
Mary Poppins, a crustacean Maria von Trapp. When
the barnacles hatch, the crab releases the parasites into
the surf, helpfully stirring up the water with its claws
to speed them on their way— *(Makes "crab claws" and
stirs)* —The cycle continues.

(Lighting change places TRENT *in the same pool of light as*
GARRETT *in* GARRETT's *bedroom.* GARRETT *is wearing a
robe.)*

GARRETT: You're the scientist—you tell me.

TRENT: About hormones?

GARRETT: A frequent topic these days.

TRENT: Bowen overdosing?

GARRETT: No, not that. Me, underdosing. Emotions
come from rushes of hormones, right?

TRENT: Sort of, yeah.

GARRETT: And hormones rush a lot more when you're
young.

TRENT: Adolescence, etcetera, right.

GARRETT: Lately, my emotions are muted, smoother
than in my youth. I'm neither depressed nor elated,
neither passionate nor pissed off. No peaks nor valleys,

just gentle rolling hills descending to a flat plain. I used to get tension— *(Points to his neck)*

TRENT: I remember.

GARRETT: But that's rare nowadays. Does that make scientific sense?

TRENT: Sure. Emotions have a purpose—

GARRETT: And I've outlived my purpose?

TRENT: No—

GARRETT: Bowen thinks he's outlived his.

TRENT: Are you concerned? About blurring emotions?

GARRETT: I can't even muster concern, really. But a certain degree of interest, I suppose.

TRENT: I'd feel relief. No more manipulation by biological imperatives.

GARRETT: Free from the manias and depressions of youth.

TRENT: Or do you miss them?

GARRETT: Some.

TRENT: How do you feel about Felix?

GARRETT: Surprised, quite frankly.

TRENT: How?

GARRETT: Surprisingly *not* muted.

TRENT: *(Placing his hand on GARRETT's shoulder)* So you haven't lost it entirely.

GARRETT: No.

TRENT: *(Massaging GARRETT's neck)* There it is. This knot is "what does Felix mean to the family?"

GARRETT: Yes.

TRENT: This is "what does Felix mean to Trent?"

GARRETT: Of course.

TRENT: This is "what does Felix mean to Garrett?"

GARRETT: A particularly embarrassing and delicate knot.

TRENT: Not as delicate as this one.

GARRETT: Which is?

TRENT: "What does Garrett mean to Trent?"

GARRETT: Ow!

TRENT: Thought so. Would you like some relief on that one?

GARRETT: If it's not too much trouble. Ooh.

TRENT: *(Massaging gently but thoroughly)* Garrett will always mean what Garrett has always meant to Trent. Garrett is the father, the rock and hiding place, a very present help in trouble, the still small voice of calm.

GARRETT: How about the burning bush? Am I still the burning bush? I'll understand if I'm not, I have reasonable expectations, you don't have to worry about that—

(TRENT silences GARRETT with a kiss on the mouth. After a moment, GARRETT returns the kiss with great passion, even a sense of desperation. The kiss breaks, they stare into each other's eyes for a moment, and then TRENT opens GARRETT's robe and begins kissing GARRETT's chest.)

GARRETT: Thank you. You don't have to, you know.

(GARRETT gasps as TRENT bites his nipple, pulling hard.)

GARRETT: Even with muted emotions—I missed you.

(TRENT kisses down GARRETT's belly toward his crotch.)

GARRETT: So much. *(Gasps)*

FELIX: *(Coming in with brochures)* Trent, you probably did all these tours a million years ago, but there's voodoo shops, cemeteries, ghosts—

(FELIX sees TRENT with GARRETT. He freezes for a moment. TRENT moves as if to hide what he's doing, then decides not to. Speechless, FELIX looks around the room, considers leaving, then speaks.)

FELIX: You told me get the brochures—

TRENT: I didn't plan on—

FELIX: —And come here!

GARRETT: Welcome to the family, Felix.

END OF ACT ONE

ACT TWO

(FELIX, TRENT, GARRETT *and* BOWEN *in separate pools of light.*)

TRENT: There's no such thing as ghosts.

FELIX: Nobody knows what ghosts are really, but they're something. They even appear in photographs—real legitimate photographic processes, not fakes. I think they're memories, past actions that get repeated. Somehow they get attached to a place, sometimes to a person. The process is probably a lot like photography, I bet. That's how we get haunted houses or people who keep seeing the same ghost again and again.

TRENT: It's a completely unscientific concept.

GARRETT: I always heard—and of course I'm very skeptical—but my understanding is ghosts are people—or more accurately *souls*—with unfinished business. They left the living world with some important work yet undone, and feel compelled to finish it. Or help others finish it. That's what I *heard*.

TRENT: Scientific investigations of "the paranormal" always prove fakery is involved. Conversations with "the dead" play on the weakness of loved ones left behind, emotionally devastated and willing to believe anything.

BOWEN: Ghosts have nothing to do with the dead. The dead do not produce energy, unless you count

decomposition, and supposed ghostly manifestations
move and glow and sometimes even knock things
around, for which energy is clearly required. The living
generate an enormous amount of energy—scientists are
only beginning to figure out how much. Poltergeists
are the best example of how living humans create
phenomena we call paranormal. Every time there's a
poltergeist knocking over furniture, there's always a
young person nearby. Usually one in psychosexual
turmoil. What spews out more energy than that, God
help us?

(Lighting changes to place BOWEN *and* FELIX *in the same
pool of light.* TRENT *remains in a separate pool.* GARRETT's
light goes out altogether.)

FELIX: *(Agitated)* Oh, my God!

TRENT:	FELIX:
Felix, that's not how I	Fuck you!
intended—	

TRENT: If you'd listen for a second—

BOWEN: *(Silencing* TRENT *with a gesture)* Young man,
may I interest you in a cemetery tour—Saint Louis
Number One? I understand you have a sentimental
attachment to graveyards.

FELIX: Not any more.

BOWEN: I could show you the Varro family vault.

FELIX: *(As* TRENT *approaches, and definitely for his benefit.)*
Mister Varro, you've said some very unpleasant things
to me, but I have to say you're the only forthright
person in your family. Trent's father was at great pains
to tell me you weren't a bunch of hillbillies, but after
growing up in the big sinful city of Los Angeles, it took
a trip to the South for me to actually *witness* father-son
incest five minutes ago—

BOWEN:	FELIX:
You shouldn't jump to—	—Involving my *boyfriend!*

TRENT: He's not my father.

FELIX: Oh, well then, that's that, all's well. However could I have gotten that tragically mistaken impression?

TRENT: Not my biological father.

(FELIX *just looks at* TRENT.)

TRENT: Garrett and I were lovers, then he adopted me for legal reasons.

FELIX: And I am?

TRENT: I'd *like* you...to be my lover as well.

FELIX: Doesn't that strike you as a wee bit greedy? You get—what?—money obviously—from Garrett, and your rocks off with me? I'm the valet, the pool boy?

TRENT: Garrett and I have a sexual relationship, too.

FELIX: Duh!! You could have told me before I cancelled appointments, lied to my boss, and dragged my tight little ass into this neogothic orgy.

TRENT: Would you have come?

FELIX: No way! Hello?!

BOWEN: Both Garrett and I agree that Trent should have been more forthcoming—he's made your visit infinitely more dramatic than necessary, as is his wont. But now that you're here, let us explain.

FELIX: You don't need to explain a thing. You're not sleeping with my boyfriend, your son is.

(BOWEN *and* TRENT *look at each other quizzically.*)

FELIX: Oh, God.

BOWEN: These days I'm sleeping with no one. However.

FELIX: What the fuck—?

TRENT: Bowen adopted Garrett just like Garrett adopted me. None of us were born Varros.

FELIX: Wait—you're *all* gay?

TRENT: Yeah.

BOWEN: Oh, Mary, thank God! My wrists were getting so stiff I thought I had arthritis!

FELIX: *(After a moment)* All that—homophobe shit was pretty elaborate.

TRENT: That—unfortunately—was not feigned.

BOWEN: Trent and I are at odds about her repressive political correctness. But Lady Hideous advised me to "tone down" my personality for your visit, so as not to scare you off.

FELIX: That was toned down?

TRENT: Practically comatose.

FELIX: But why were you so shocked when you saw Trent brought home a boy?

BOWEN: At first, my dear, simply because you're so goddamned good-looking. Most of Trent's dates look like specimens she drug outta someone's intestine. And then because Trent introduced us as her father and grandfather. I loathe lying to homosexuals. Heteros, on the other hand, don't deserve to hear the truth and wouldn't understand it if they did.

FELIX: I don't think I understand it.

TRENT: I should have told you, but I didn't want to risk you not coming.

FELIX: Anything would have been better than walking in on—

TRENT: I'm sorry—I thought—

FELIX: When I get back to L A, I'm changing my phone number, moving, and getting plastic surgery.

TRENT: But—

BOWEN: That's all perfectly reasonable.

TRENT: But—

BOWEN: But in the meantime, why waste a visit to America's most haunted city? I could show you the tomb of Marie Laveau, the voodoo priestess.

FELIX: No thanks, but where can I buy a doll?

BOWEN: Trent, you're a tad unpopular at the moment. Why don't you stay home and I'll play cruise director for the unhappy Felix this afternoon?

TRENT: Shit.

BOWEN: You can't control every experiment, Trent.

TRENT: Felix—

BOWEN: Trust me, my dear, I couldn't possibly fuck up the situation further. Could I?

(Lights out on TRENT *and up on* LENDELL, *the tour guide for the Ghosts of New Orleans Tour. After a few moments* FELIX *and* BOWEN *join him.)*

LENDELL: New Orleans has one of the highest murder rates in the country, second only to our nation's capital. Therefore, it's only natural that we have more hauntings than any other city. Most buildings in New Orleans are hundreds of years old and have housed many generations—living and dead. *(Gesturing)* Built in 1755 by a sugar cane grower, this residence has seen its share of tragedies. Slaves suffered here, several children and a few adults died of yellow fever, and at least two murders were committed. Paranormal investigators have identified seven troubled spirits: a man, a woman, four children, and something else.

FELIX: Something else?

LENDELL: The children are innocents, looking for their parents, for help, for love. The woman protects them from the man, who apparently wishes them harm. But they all fear something else, some kind of malevolent presence, which may have been responsible for the tragic history of this house. *(Smiles)* It rarely manifests, so we should be safe today.

FELIX: How does it manifest?

LENDELL: When this house was first built, there was a bell tower. The bell was rung in times of war, during epidemics, emergencies. Burned down more than a hundred years ago, but they say the malevolent presence tolls the ghostly bell when tragedy looms for someone in the house. *(Cheerfully)* Follow me to the attic—that's where we usually find the children. *(Disappears.)*

FELIX: This is very cool. Thanks for insisting.

BOWEN: It's all ridiculous, but I got a little shiver, didn't you?

FELIX: So you like ghosts, too?

BOWEN: Of course. I very nearly *am* one.

FELIX: Don't you just love the idea of this secret world existing all around us, that most of us can't see? Seven ghosts here, Marie Laveau lurking there—imagine if we all had the ability to tap into that. I believe we did, long ago, back in cave-man days, but evolved out of it.

BOWEN: For God's sake, don't spout that nonsense to Trent!

FELIX: I don't care what he thinks. I like my secret world. I want to see more of it.

BOWEN: We've made our own secret world, you know.

FELIX: What do you mean?

BOWEN: Our family. I don't suppose Trent has told you any of our tenets?

FELIX: Tenets? He told me *nada*.

BOWEN: When it's time for the youngest partner—in this case, Trent—to bring someone new into the fold, he knows he must find just the right kind of young man. Preferably one with no family, accomplished but not flashy—we don't want to call attention to ourselves—and with a great generosity of spirit.

FELIX: Someone willing to share.

BOWEN: And worth sharing.

(FELIX *looks away*.)

BOWEN: We've all had to give up a few things. Garrett would prefer to work on modernist architecture, but there's not much of that in New Orleans so he restores traditional homes and estates. Trent can roam a bit chasing worms and weevils, although that's hard on Garrett, who knows his place is here with me, the oldest living member.

FELIX: You guys have a ton of money—why not just hire some twink to take care of you?

BOWEN: Oh, how awfully shallow. Besides knowing that he'll inherit everything, Garrett's motivated by love. That's why he stays with me—a much greater comfort than some twenty year-old gold-digger.

FELIX: Now I'm a gold-digger?

BOWEN: If I thought you were, I wouldn't waste time on this conversation. Trent's not one either—he could give a fuck about the money, in fact—but he knows when Garrett becomes the oldest, Trent's place will be with him.

FELIX: You got it all worked out, in a creepy kinda way.

BOWEN: Tested by time. A secret world within a secret world.

FELIX: The gay world isn't secret any more.

BOWEN: You don't find it rather delicious that queens can walk down the street making eye contact with other fairies, completely communicating our desires, our essence, and hets have no idea?

FELIX: Men and women do that too—it's not just us.

BOWEN: They're so blatant about it! But homo dramas play out under their noses all the time. In a public men's room, a straight man comes in to take a dump, barely noticing the other men in cubicles and at urinals. He does his foul business, rudely stinking up the place, and departs. The second he's gone, everyone's back on their knees, straining against porcelain, shaking the walls of the stalls. And all of it communicated without a word.

FELIX: That's your generation, not mine. Secrecy's unhealthy, spreads disease.

BOWEN: I think you find us fascinating or you wouldn't still be here. Like your secret ghost world. In the harsh light of day, beauty disappears.

FELIX: I wanna kiss a guy in public, I do it. No big deal.

BOWEN: Good God—what's the fun in that?

FELIX: You tell me.

(FELIX *kisses* BOWEN *on the mouth.*)

BOWEN: Don't trifle with me, boy.

FELIX: Lots of ways to be creepy.

LENDELL: *(Appearing)* Not creepy at all. They're very affectionate and rather sweet. Often they want to hold visitors' hands. Do you notice a cold spot around your fingers? *(Feels the air near* FELIX*'s hand)* Yes, oh,

definitely, that's probably the little girl. She's shy at
first, but once she finds someone she likes, she doesn't
want to let go. Do you feel it?

FELIX: Maybe a little coolness.

LENDELL: *(Feeling near* FELIX's *other hand)* Here, too. The
older boy stays with the girl, so he's taking your other
hand.

FELIX: *(Standing stiffly holding hands with invisible
children)* You think?

LENDELL: *(Feeling the air near* BOWEN*)* Why, Mister
Varro, they seem to like you, too.

BOWEN: *(Batting at the air around his hands)* Ugh! Go
away! Little brats!

LENDELL: *(Continues to feel the air)* They're still here.
(Holds up a hand) I've got one, too. I think it's the
woman. They're particularly needy today. This cold is
very intense.

FELIX: I'm really feeling it.

BOWEN: Felix, stop.

FELIX: My hair's standing up. Is the man coming?

LENDELL: Maybe—

BOWEN: *(Clasping himself for warmth)* This is absurd!

LENDELL: Or perhaps it's—

BOWEN, FELIX & LENDELL: Something else?

*(An eerie bell peals. They all freeze and look up. Instant
lighting change isolates* BOWEN *and plunges the other two
into darkness.)*

BOWEN: When I was nineteen I decided if sex ever
became impossible, I would kill myself. Now it has,
and I haven't. Which is astonishing to me. All my life,
I've been—voracious. Cautiously so, quietly so, but
certainly so. I do apologize, Lady Hideous, for this

medically mandated menopause. With Trent across the country, I'm sure you're missing sex as much as I am not. My gash has healed right up, airtight. But I cherish our conversations and hope you do as well. Try not to think about it. While these cunty hormones shrink my balls and restore my hair, I find I'd rather listen to Aaron Copeland or whip up an etouffee.

GARRETT: *(Appearing, having changed from* LENDELL*)* Or have a Sazerac.

BOWEN: Well, of course.

GARRETT: *(Starting to mix a drink)* Would you like one?

BOWEN: No, I'll be strong.

GARRETT: I won't.

BOWEN: I spent the afternoon with Felix.

GARRETT: I can't even look at him.

BOWEN: *(Giggles)* Wish I'd been there for your little tableau.

GARRETT: I'm sure you do.

BOWEN: He's overly earnest.

GARRETT: But?

BOWEN: And a little odd. All that ghost shit.

GARRETT: But?

BOWEN: I find I'm falling for him.

*(*GARRETT *stares.)*

BOWEN: In a perfectly appropriate way. Only the limp lust I'm permitted since my gelding. I think he's right for Trent. And for us. I intend to encourage them.

GARRETT: I can't.

BOWEN: Will you believe me when I say I understand?

GARRETT: I'm sure you do. This is very much after the fact, but I'd like to apologize.

BOWEN: For?

GARRETT: Trent.

BOWEN: What's he done now?

GARRETT: No, what I did—then. When I met him.

BOWEN: I did the same when I met you. Rudy understood.

GARRETT: Rudy was very good about it. You were very good about it.

BOWEN: We had to be.

GARRETT: I don't think I can be.

BOWEN: You're not losing a son, you're gaining a grandson.

GARRETT: Flippant!

BOWEN: Apologies. But I'm obligated to goad you into action. You're undoubtedly a better emissary than I—you're the competition.

(GARRETT *looks unconvinced.*)

BOWEN: Are you afraid he'll never touch you again?

GARRETT: Yes.

(*Lights up on* TRENT *seated at an ancient bar. Thumping dance music in the background, almost subliminal. Dancing upon the bar clumsily, but undeniably sexily, is* TOD, *played by the same actor as* FELIX. *He's wearing threadbare cut-off shorts and work boots.* TRENT *is looking at the gravestone rubbing with his and* FELIX's *names on it.*)

BOWEN: Are you afraid they'll giggle about you when they're alone?

GARRETT: I wasn't, but thanks, now I am.

BOWEN: Are you afraid you'll be one generation nearer to Saint Louis Number One?

GARRETT: You're still first in line. But yes, it does bump me closer behind you.

(TRENT *delicately attempts to put a five- dollar bill in* TOD's *cut-offs.* TOD *grabs* TRENT's *hand and grinds it into his crotch.* TRENT *does not resist.*)

BOWEN: Are you afraid they'll fall so much in love Trent will leave you—leave us—altogether and run off to L A never to return? Are you imagining your pathetic quest for a new Trent at your age? Imagining yourself completely ignored while everyone's fondling a stripper at the Corner Pocket?

(GARRETT *says nothing.*)

BOWEN: You see? I do understand. It could be worse. Imagine me trying to find a new you at my age? Come hold me, Grandpa. Great Grandpa's paved the road before you with his tears.

(*Lights fade on* BOWEN *and* GARRETT *as they embrace. The dance music bumps up to full volume then changes tunes.* TOD *jumps off the bar.*)

TOD: (*Grabbing* TRENT *by the hand*) C'mon, baby! It's my break!

(TOD *drags* TRENT *outside to a wall. The music fades to a lower volume and crickets are heard.*)

TOD: (*Pressing up against* TRENT. *Street lingo mixed with a heavy country accent.*) Hot night.

TRENT: Pretty warm, yes. You, too. Hot, I mean.

TOD: What you doin' in the Corner Pocket? You the only guy in there under ninety. Tourist?

TRENT: No, I'm from here, sort of.

TOD: Got somewheres we can go?

TRENT: No, actually.

TOD: No biggie. I got a arrangement with my buddy at a motel on Rampart. Thirty-five dollars.

TRENT: Don't you have another set? Or dance, or whatever?

TOD: Not for forty-five minutes, so we got almost a hour.

(TRENT *hesitates.*)

TOD: Aw, c'mon, you're not gonna get cheap on me now, are ya? Only thirty-five dollars. *(Grabs the cemetery rubbing)*

TRENT: Hey!

TOD: *(Reading the rubbing)* You Felix?

TRENT: Trent. Give it back.

TOD: You look like a Felix. Come and get it, Trent.

(TOD *and* TRENT *start walking.*)

TOD: You party?

TRENT: I...have sex, if that's what you mean. Can I have that back?

TOD: No, *party.* Got any crystal?

TRENT: Oh, no.

TOD: G?

TRENT: No, sorry.

TOD: X?

TRENT: Definitely not.

TOD: S'okay, I got a little. Only twenty-five bucks.

TRENT: That's all right. I'm not into it.

TOD: Baby, I can't do it unless I'm tweaking.

TRENT: Do what?

TOD: You're not following me just to get this— *(Waves the cemetery rubbing then shoves it in his pants)* —Are you?

TRENT: *(Caught)* No.

TOD: Good—only twenty-five for the crystal, like I said.

TRENT: But you already have it.

TOD: Right.

TRENT: So why don't you just give it—to yourself?

TOD: Part of the whole, you know, experience, man. You paying for the whole burrito.

TRENT: And how much total for the...burrito?

TOD: Baby, you can add: twenty-five for the crystal, thirty-five for the room—

TRENT: *(Stops walking)* Where exactly is this motel?

TOD: Rampart.

TRENT: We're *on* Rampart.

TOD: *(Dragging TRENT)* 'Nother couple blocks.

TRENT: *(Resumes walking)* I don't see it.

TOD: Down there. Cheap-asses never fix their neon.

TRENT: You know, this isn't the greatest neighborhood to be walking in. Maybe a taxi—

TOD: It's cool. You with me.

TRENT: Okay, not to be tacky, but beyond the room and the drugs, how much is this gonna cost me?

TOD: Baby, don't be talkin' money on the street! Later for that.

TRENT: Yeah, but I wanna make sure I got enough.

TOD: You a cop?

TRENT: No!

TOD: Comin' up on a A T M.

TRENT: *(Reaching for his wallet)* No, I've got—I think I can—if you'll just tell me—

TOD: *(Grabbing at* TRENT's *wallet)* Don't be diggin' in your wallet in public, man!

TRENT: *(Shoves wallet back in his pocket, stops dead still)* How much?

TOD: Baby, c'mon.

*(*TRENT *holds his ground.)*

TOD: Hundred. And that's giving it away. Okay? Now, c'mon.

*(*TOD *and* TRENT *start walking again.)*

TOD: Not a good locale for contestin' the pricin' y'understand? 'Round here niggers sooner gut you than look at you.

*(*TOD *and* TRENT *walk in silence for a bit.)*

TRENT: For this—*amount*—what do you do, exactly?

TOD: Baby!

TRENT: Is that a blow-job? A hand-job? Do I get to fuck you?

TOD: Fuck me? You gotta be kiddin'. I'm straight, man.

TRENT: *(Stops)* Straight!?

TOD: Shut up, baby! You wanna get shot right here on Rampart?

TRENT: Okay, you're straight. Does that mean you fuck me?

TOD: For 'nother fifty I'll pound your tight little ass till it squeaks. Gimme some money and I get us some lube.

TRENT: Uh…you know, I'm tired of the math. Maybe we better just—

TOD: Naw, man, calm down. Make it thirty.

TRENT: I wasn't planning—

TOD: Okay, Jew me down—I'll fuck you for a hundred. Plus motel and—

TRENT: I'm gonna go. Sorry.

TOD: No tweaking required! How's that? Practically free!

TRENT: *(Edging away)* Sorry to waste your time.

TOD: I gotta make something! Be fair.

TRENT:	TOD:
Sorry, sorry—good night.	Baby!
(Starts to walk away)	

TOD: Dragged me 'cross the Quarter—! For nuthin'! *(Following)* Better watch your ass, cocksucker.

*(*TRENT *speeds up. So does* TOD. *They disappear. Lights up on* ROBERT *in the middle of his spiel. He's played by the same actor as* BOWEN. *He's drinking a hurricane from a large plastic cup. It's almost gone and so is he.)*

ROBERT: I hope ya'll've enjoyed our little tour of gay New Orleans as much as I have. You've seen oppression, such as the firebombing of our most popular bar— *(Sucks on his straw)* —And resistance in the form of havens lesbian and gay people have made for ourselves over time, such as Lafitte's. I always like to conclude our tour here, in this quaint and— *(Burps or hiccoughs)* —Charming little alley in the shadow of Saint Louis Cathedral. I want to honor our lesbian and gay brothers and sisters of the past by calling on their spirits to join us here— *(Waves his hands in an invoking, welcoming gesture, almost spilling his drink)* —Behind the church.

(Lights up on TRENT *and* FELIX *observing the tour with* GARRETT *between them.)*

ROBERT: I invite all men, women and those uncommitted to a gender to grace us with their gentle presence, filling this space with their love. Men loving men, women loving women, uncommitteds loving... whomever they wish to love. Do you feel it? Do you feel the love?

(FELIX *gives himself over to the experience, closing his eyes and raising his hands slightly in a tentative gesture of invocation.* TRENT *and* GARRETT *look at him and at each other.*)

ROBERT: *(Starts getting teary-eyed)* Next week and next year and on into the future, when I invite the spirits of our brothers and sisters, I'll be inviting you, too.

(ROBERT *grabs their hands. They reluctantly form a circle.*)

ROBERT: Please come. Please fill this alley with your love as we remember *your* life and *your* accomplishments and *your* suffering for daring to love. *(Raises his hands over his head to feel the air)* They're here—I feel them—all around us, the alley is full of love. Can you feel it? *(Almost sobbing)* So much love—I—pardon me—

GARRETT: Robert—

ROBERT: *(Tears streaming down his face)* I'm sorry, Garrett. I just get over— *(Hiccoughs or burps)* — Whelmed—

GARRETT: *(His arm around* ROBERT, *but rolling his eyes at* TRENT*)* It's okay, Robert. We understand. It's very moving to think about.

ROBERT: Especially seeing you and Trent— *(Touches* TRENT*)* It's been ages. You and your dad mean a lot to me, to this community—

FELIX: Thank you. This has been great.

ROBERT: I'm so encouraged when young queerlings take an interest. Gives me hope. Can you feel the spirits?

FELIX: Yes.

ROBERT: And will you come back when I call you, will your spirit return?

FELIX: Always.

ROBERT: *(To* GARRETT*)* Thank Bowen for me—people love seeing where Tennessee wrote, and Bowen gave me such good anecdotes about your house being a "specialty" bordello.

GARRETT: Speaking of Bowen, he's expecting me, and Trent has to give a lecture at Tulane.

ROBERT: Of course, Garrett. Good to see you both. And so nice to meet you, young man.

FELIX: Nice to meet you.

TRENT: Bye, Robert.

GARRETT: Take care, Robert—you need us to walk you home?

ROBERT: No—I'm fine—the spirits will guide me!

*(*ROBERT *waves good-bye as the light goes out on him.* TRENT, FELIX, *and* GARRETT *start walking.)*

FELIX: Thank you—that was amazing!

GARRETT: He breaks down like that every time.

TRENT: 'Cause he always gives the tour liquored-up.

GARRETT: It's embarrassing.

FELIX: I loved it. He's very sincere and sweet.

TRENT: He's gonna be all right staggering home? It'll be dark soon.

GARRETT: He drags himself home drunk several times a week. It's his natural state. I'm more worried about Bowen.

TRENT: That's his natural state, too.

GARRETT: Don't speak of him like that.

TRENT: Sorry.

GARRETT: He's dealing with a lot right now. Claims he's bored. Tired of it all.

TRENT: That why you're worried?

GARRETT: That and this suspicious character hanging around outside the house late last night. I turned on all the outside lights and he finally left.

FELIX: Do you need us to come with you?

GARRETT: No, it's fine. I doubt he'll come back.

TRENT: Are you planning to come to the lecture?

FELIX: I like your lectures. It's you I have a problem with.

TRENT: Okay, but no heckling.

FELIX: Like I owe you a promise!

(Lighting change puts TRENT *alone at a lectern)*

TRENT: We need our parasites. Over millions of years of co-evolution, our bodies and theirs are perfectly adapted to each other in a passionate love/hate relationship. We simply can't live without these tiny hustlers. We've tried, and the results—in some cases— have been disastrous. Until about the middle of the twentieth century, almost no one got colitis or Crohn's disease, conditions in which the body's immune system attacks the lining of the intestine. More than a million Americans suffer from these diseases today, but who are they? Primarily the upper to middle class: people who drink clean water, wash their food, and get good medical care. People without intestinal worms. Deprived of its traditional enemies, the immune system attacks its own body. In some cases, colitis and Crohn's disease have been cured by the re-introduction of parasites to their natural environment—us.

FELIX: *(In the audience)* Damn, that son of a bitch is good.

TRENT: Let's broaden, for a moment, our definition of parasites. Assuming they are necessary, co-dependent, symbiotic, who else might be a parasite? *(Glances toward* FELIX*)*

FELIX: Okay, where are you going?

TRENT: Am I, a gay man, a parasite of heterosexual society?

FELIX: Oh, my God!

TRENT: Like cowbirds, homosexuals trick heterosexuals into raising their young. If the main purpose of a species is to pass on its genes, we're an absolute detriment to *homo sapiens*. We deliberately seek the least fertile places to sow our seed.

FELIX: Queers as parasites? Holy shit!

TRENT: Yet gay genes continue from generation to generation. Why would this extinction-inducing trait thrive? Why are there still homosexuals? Surely not just to design a fabulous gown or a spectacular cathedral, although these are lovely collateral benefits.

FELIX: Clichés! Trent, no!

TRENT: Like other parasites, we must have evolved a purpose that serves the host species. I'll ask you to contemplate what that might be until tomorrow's lecture, but consider this: the incidence of homosexuality rises as a population grows. Thank you, and don't forget to feed your parasites! You might want to try to the pork tenderloin in the student union cafeteria—it smelled deliciously undercooked.

(Lighting change as FELIX *joins* TRENT.*)*

FELIX: I know it was my suggestion, but was that the best way—?

TRENT: Sorry if that was awkward. I never came out in a lecture before, and the dean looked pissed.

FELIX: *(Gestures separation)* Your work—and your life.

TRENT: *(Gestures bringing them together, making a sound effect)* Your fault.

FELIX: I'm still taking a different plane.

TRENT: Don't.

FELIX: Why do you want me so badly? You've only known me three days.

TRENT: This isn't the first time I've tried this, you know. I'm not a kid—you're well aware of that. I've seen enough guys to know what I want.

FELIX: You've drug other guys to New Orleans and tested them in the fires of hell?

TRENT: You're the first to make it this far.

FELIX: But, why me? And why'd you hide so much?

TRENT: When I was up-front with other guys, all they saw was the family money.

FELIX: That was my first sign to run away.

TRENT: And my first sign to chase you. You don't care about the money, you resent the money. I hate it, too. Always have.

FELIX: It's like prostitution! You've been sent out to purchase the next generation.

TRENT: I know you can't be bought. That's what I love about you.

FELIX: Please don't say that. It's flippant.

(TRENT *smiles.*)

FELIX: What?

TRENT: That's a Garrett word.

FELIX: You still love him, don't you?

TRENT: Yes.

FELIX: So you can't really *love* me.

TRENT: If I was cagey, I'd say no of course not, not yet, how could I possibly on such short acquaintance, you can't hurry love, you just have to wait, it's a game of give and take. But you see what happens when I'm cagey.

FELIX: Things get fucked up. Bad. So…what you're saying is…?

TRENT: I'd like you to be my…son.

FELIX: You know, this would be a real easy decision either way except for one thing. Totally easy for me to just jump on a plane and tell all my friends in L A how freaky folks are in New Orleans. Or just as easy for me to say okay nothing wrong with being taken care of the rest of my life so I'd have time to collect ghost stories and write books. Even if it means surrendering my nubile form to a couple of older gentlemen every once in a while—I'm assuming that's expected, yes?

TRENT: It helps.

FELIX: It's like Frenching the dead! Don't you find this whole arrangement completely bizarre? You figured out how to cheat the world, how to sidestep hetero hegemony, but I keep waiting for the other shoe to drop. For Rod Serling to pop in and render poetic justice for your hubris.

TRENT: Felix, it's not without its bumps, but this has worked for a very long time.

FELIX: How long?

TRENT: It's not just me, Garrett, and Bowen. Before that there was Rudy—

FELIX: This has been going on for what—generations?

TRENT: Kinda like a dynasty.

FELIX: But you don't have to do this any more. This— dynasty—is a reactionary survival mechanism for a world that no longer exists. A tiny world you can control where everybody knows everybody else, for safety's sake. An old world where survival meant secrecy. Bowen actually likes sneaking around in the dark like some kind of ghost. Nowadays silence equals death, dude, to quote your generation. I come from a big world, an open world. I don't want to make my world small again.

TRENT: Help us open our world then, if that's the problem.

FELIX: None of that's the problem.

TRENT: What is?

FELIX: I'm old enough to know what I want, too.

TRENT: Which is?

FELIX: You. Alone. I don't want to share.

(Lights fade on FELIX *and* TRENT *as* BOWEN *calls out plaintively as the lights on him slowly rise. He's wearing his robe and fixing a drink.)*

BOWEN: *Flores! Flores para los pendejos!* The most godawful production of *Streetcar Named Desire* I've ever seen! I doubt you're rushing off to buy tickets, but I won't allow you to even consider it. *(Drinks)* The director had an inspired idea: a black Blanche. He even

renamed the character: Noir Dubois. A long program
note about casting against type. Directors who write
program notes should write their own goddamn
plays. *(Drinks)* I'm sorry, terribly sorry—that's not at
all what I wanted to talk about. I mostly just want to
apologize. Don't interrupt, please, or it'll never come
out. At the end of one's life, one thinks about tidying
things up. We live a rather tidy life as it is, except for a
few dangling threads, some uncatalogued remnants. I
won't say I feel guilty for abducting you from Arizona,
but I do realize what you've given up. I took you
away from the Taliesen community, a brotherhood,
practically a cult, and initiated you into another. You
loved modern design, clean lines, and I brought you—
rococo. Complicated, overdone, messy. Ancient houses
covered in vines, warped, teetering drunkenly on the
verge of collapse, and you're the savior. You sneak
in an I-beam here, pour a foundation there, the old
plantation is propped up ready for the tourists, and the
kudzu never even rustled. *(Drinks)* I am…immensely
grateful. Have I ever said so? Immensely. I'm partial
to beauty, and beauty's what you do, what you *are*. It's
my weakness—and don't say "one of many" because
all my other flaws stem from this one—I sacrifice
everything for beauty. Our family, our dynasty, is our
most beautiful creation, well, not our creation, but ours
to preserve, to conserve, to renovate. I am aware of
your sacrifice. I am aware of your beauty. Why else do
you suppose I call you Lady Hideous? What else can I
do in the face of such beauty?

(Lights up on TOD, *listening impatiently. He holds an empty
glass.)*

TOD: Baby, I know I'm hot—guys tell me every damn
day.

BOWEN: Shhh!

TOD: And I ain't never been to no Arizona!

BOWEN: Please!

TOD: You about done? Gonna suck me off or what?

BOWEN: *(Sighs)* I'm done.

TOD: *(Unbuttoning trousers)* I had plenty of time before you ate it up talking.

BOWEN: Button up, please.

TOD: Huh?

BOWEN: No need to drop trou.

TOD: After all that—?

BOWEN: You've been very helpful. Thank you for your kind attention.

TOD: I got no idea what you said.

BOWEN: That's fine. Scamper back to your hole.

TOD: Soon's you pay up.

BOWEN: Pay up?

TOD: Charge is the same, sucking or no.

BOWEN: Oh my, did you think—?

TOD: Old man, don't play that.

BOWEN: I invited you in for a glass of cherry limeade. Cool you off and make your mouth all sweet.

TOD: A hundred dollars—I told you!

BOWEN: I'm sorry if I misunderstood.

TOD: *(Throws the glass to the floor, breaking it.)* Understand this!

BOWEN: My Philippe Starck!

TOD: *(Forcing a shard of glass to BOWEN's throat)* Gonna break a lot more than glass if you don't pay up!

BOWEN: It's okay—it was from Target.

TOD: I know you got it. All this— *(Gestures around the room.)* —art and shit—

BOWEN: Would you settle for a small Paul Cadmus drawing?

(Sound of a key in the door. BOWEN *and* TOD *react to the sound.)*

TOD: Motherfuck!

(Lights out simultaneously with the sound of the sinister bell. It tolls several times in darkness, then the lights come up on TRENT *dressed in mourning clothes. He stands almost motionless as the bell tolls, holding back emotion. The bell stops and suddenly a jazz band strikes up a lively tune: it's a New Orleans jazz funeral. After a few moments of music,* TRENT *begins to smile, perhaps to laugh.* FELIX *shows up, also in mourning attire.)*

FELIX: You okay?

TRENT: Think so.

FELIX: Why're you laughing?

TRENT: I have no idea. *(Glances at* FELIX*)* Overnight tailoring worked out.

FELIX: I always look good in black.

TRENT: Yes, you do. Thanks for staying.

FELIX: Pretty fancy funeral.

TRENT: New Orleans is good with death.

FELIX: Pricey, I mean. Other people don't rate funerals like this.

TRENT: We're an old family. That means something here.

FELIX: Even this kind of family?

TRENT: Especially this kind. *(Pause)* I'll tell you why I was laughing.

FELIX: Why?

TRENT: I keep thinking about angler fish.

FELIX: Angler fish?

TRENT: They live at the bottom of the ocean, in the dark, completely adapted to the cold and enormous pressure. They're jet black, but the female—about— *(Gestures—size of a cantaloupe)* —Yea big—has this little phosphorescent light she dangles out in from of her— *(Demonstrates)* —to lure prey.

FELIX: What makes you think of that?

TRENT: The male—this big— *(Gestures—size of a jelly bean)* —when he finds a female down there in the dark, doesn't want to lose her, so he bites onto her— *(Demonstrates on his face)* —and hangs on for the rest of his life. Eventually their circulatory systems merge and he's absorbed into her body until he's nothing but a pimple, really.

FELIX: Or a parasite?

TRENT: In the broadest sense.

FELIX: Or the two halves of the soul—

TRENT: But I never thought about what happens when one of them dies. Do they both die, like Siamese twins?

FELIX: She's the bigger half, so she'd probably survive his death, but he's so small—

TRENT: He probably wouldn't make it if she died.

FELIX: *(Seeing someone in the distance)* Oh, here comes—

TRENT: Don't—

FELIX: Shouldn't we—?

TRENT: No. I think he's all right.

BOWEN: *(Entering with true dignity, in mourning. Completely sober)* Garrett had a lot of clients.

TRENT: Friends.

BOWEN: I wonder whether he would find a jazz funeral acceptable.

TRENT: Why are you late?

BOWEN: Police.

FELIX: Any idea...who...?

BOWEN: No.

TRENT: Just another queer with his throat slit.

BOWEN: Don't use that word.

TRENT: Like you should talk!

BOWEN: Garrett hated that word. Said it was like being kicked in the stomach.

TRENT: No idea at all?

FELIX: You never saw the guy?

BOWEN: An intruder, a burglar—I told them, I told you. I heard noises, locked myself in my room—

TRENT: And you saw *nothing*?

BOWEN: Trent, I just went through this with the police. I am by no means brave.

TRENT: Sorry. *(Suppresses a sob)*

FELIX: Trent, it's okay, go ahead. You don't have to be a scientist all the time.

BOWEN: Garrett would prefer that we not.

FELIX: Not cry?

BOWEN: Not here. Not in front of everyone.

TRENT: He wasn't—ready.

FELIX: You afraid people will guess?

BOWEN: It's our business.

FELIX: A son can't cry at his father's funeral—?

BOWEN: You can do that at home.

FELIX: A father can't cry at his son's—?

TRENT: You—were ready.

BOWEN: Please stop.

FELIX: They all know! Nudge, nudge, wink, wink—
they *know*.

BOWEN: But I don't *know* they know.

TRENT: And you saw *nothing*!

FELIX: Who are you protecting?

BOWEN: The family, young man.

FELIX: What kind of family can't cry at a funeral?

BOWEN: I didn't expect Garrett to cry at my funeral. I
didn't cry at Rudy's. Rudy didn't at Hammet's funeral.
Hammet didn't cry when Anton passed. Anton didn't
when Cyrus was killed, yes, murdered here in our
number two in the nation homicide city. Cyrus didn't
cry for Aaron. Aaron didn't cry for Beauchamp.
Beauchamp didn't cry for Jean-Paul. Jean-Paul didn't
cry for Etienne—

FELIX: *(Overlapping)* Wait—

BOWEN: Etienne didn't cry for Cesar. Cesar didn't cry
for Claude—

FELIX: How many generations—?

BOWEN: Claude didn't cry for Philippe. Philippe didn't
cry for Marcel—

FELIX: Stop, please—

BOWEN: Marcel didn't cry for—

FELIX: *(Urgently but not too loud)* Stop!

(BOWEN stops.)

FELIX: How many generations of men…didn't cry? Altogether? How far back?

BOWEN: I've never counted, really.

FELIX: To the French Revolution?

BOWEN: Oh, before, that's why we came—that was Cesar—

TRENT: Claude.

BOWEN: I get them mixed up.

FELIX: Further? The Sun King?

BOWEN: Well established at that point. Vineyards, mostly.

FELIX: Agincourt?

BOWEN: We were Italian then. Right, Trent?

TRENT: Lombards, actually.

FELIX: Petrarch?

TRENT: Further.

FELIX: Constantine?

BOWEN: You're getting warmer.

FELIX: Come on, guys, Homer?

BOWEN: Now you've overshot.

TRENT: Varro is a Roman name.

FELIX: Rome—Roman? Roman Empire Roman?

BOWEN: The Republic, actually.

TRENT: Roman law allowed adult adoption—

FELIX: You expect me to believe that for more than two thousand years—

BOWEN: You don't have to believe it. We believe it.

TRENT: It's all written down. We have an archive.

FELIX: No tears…for two thousand years—that's what you're protecting—

BOWEN: That's how we've survived a hostile environment. We adapted.

(Silence for a moment as FELIX *absorbs this.)*

BOWEN: Shall we go?

FELIX: Yeah, Trent, maybe we should go.

TRENT: Okay, let's go—

BOWEN: Yes—home—you can cry there if you like.

TRENT: I don't want to.

BOWEN: Cry? Good.

TRENT: I don't want to go back.

BOWEN: Felix, will you drive?

TRENT: I want to go to Los Angeles.

(Lighting change so that TRENT *is alone at a lectern.)*

TRENT: One of the most important life principles— if you're a parasite—is that of optimal virulence. Just how much can you take from the host—how much food, how much blood—before you kill it? Killing the host often means the parasite dies as well. If tapeworms ate all our food, if hookworms sucked all our blood, we'd die and so would they. Self-regulation is important for all species, not just parasites. There is, however, one species notable for its lack of self-regulation: *homo sapiens.* We're close to fishing out the oceans, polluting all potable water, and destroying the forests and plankton that provide the very air we breathe. The earth is our host, and we are its parasite—a parasite that has far exceeded optimal virulence. Nature tries to fight back. Lurking unknown in the African jungle until forty years ago, AIDS has killed or afflicted more than fifty-eight

million worldwide. Overcrowded parts of the world
have always been vulnerable to epidemics like cholera,
yellow fever and the Black Death. I'm sure Mother
Nature has worse viruses up her sleeve, ready to
regulate her most destructive children. Social ills
also increase in overcrowded conditions—suicide,
infanticide, child abuse, and patricide— *(Pauses
for a moment to take a deep breath)* —All terribly—
unfortunate—but remarkably effective means of
reducing the surplus population. Violence is in our
blood—the omnivorous diet that fueled our remarkable
brain size also programmed us to kill—and when there
are too many of us, we—kill ourselves. But evolution
is smarter than we are, and has provided us with some
less horrific forms of regulation. In my last lecture I
mentioned that the incidence of homosexuality rises
as populations become overcrowded. Homosexuals
are—*we* are—an evolutionary advantage to our species,
a non-violent alternative to—to— *(Pause)* I'm sorry.
I'm—uh—I'm going to have to cut this short. You see,
my fa—my, my *lover*, Garrett Varro, was murdered
three days ago, so the topic hits a little close to home,
and— *(Takes a moment to compose himself)* Evolution of
species takes place imperceptibly over eons. But social
evolution can happen in a relative blink of an eye.
Homosexuality only got a name a hundred years ago.
It only became a movement between fifty and sixty
years ago with the Mattachine Society. It only came out
of the closet forty years ago with the Stonewall riots. It
only garnered national sympathy almost thirty years
ago with the advent of AIDS. What did your father
think of homosexuality? Your father's father? Society is
slowly figuring it out—our counter-evolutionary and
anti-reproductive trait keeps popping up in our genes
for a reason. We are not an accident, a fluke—we help
the species survive. Today's lecture was supposed
to be about parasites. It seems I've gotten off track.

Perhaps not. Perhaps all of us—all human beings—are truly parasites. *(Singing to the tune of People.)* And parasites, parasites who need parasites Are the luckiest parasites in the world!

(Instant lighting change puts TRENT *alone with* FELIX.*)*

TRENT: I figured it out. He's protecting someone.

FELIX: Bowen is?

TRENT: Someone gay. There's no way he could have avoided witnessing—but he's holding back, I can tell he's holding back. He's not just protecting the family by staying in the closet, he's refusing to turn in a gay murderer.

FELIX: Who killed his lover, his son?

TRENT: I think he hates straight people—the police—even more.

FELIX: Hates straight people?

*(*BOWEN *appears.)*

TRENT & BOWEN: Don't you?

FELIX: No! Don't you think— *(A glance to* TRENT*)* —you owe Garrett a measure of justice?

BOWEN: Justice! Whenever in the world has there been justice? There is only retribution answering retribution, with the vanquisher declaring justice.

TRENT: If you know—

BOWEN: I don't.

FELIX: If you *knew*—

TRENT: Anything.

FELIX: Anything.

*(*BOWEN *says nothing.)*

TRENT: If it's someone gay—

(BOWEN *says nothing.*)

TRENT: If you're protecting someone gay, or if you're embarrassed—

BOWEN: Embarrassed! Garrett's been killed—what's embarrassment to that?

TRENT: I know you sometimes have—young men—come to visit. Garrett knew, I knew, no big deal. If it was one of those—

BOWEN: What in the world good would it do? Retribution—another life destroyed—

TRENT: Whoever killed Garrett could—

FELIX: —Do something similar—

TRENT: —To someone else.

FELIX: Not retribution—prevention.

BOWEN: I'm sorry. I don't know.

TRENT: Mendacity! I think you do. (*Glances at* FELIX) And if I thought that you'd—hide—

FELIX: Trent's prepared—

TRENT: Felix—! I can—

FELIX: Okay, okay.

TRENT: I couldn't stay, Bowen. I'm sorry, but I couldn't. Felix says I can stay with him in California—

BOWEN: The day we're honoring Garrett's memory, you'd let us go extinct?

TRENT: No—extinct—I'm sure—

FELIX: Yes. Yes, he would.

BOWEN: My premonition's come true.

TRENT: Would there really be anything left to die out?

BOWEN: Me.

TRENT: You can find someone to take care of you.
You're in remission. The money always—

BOWEN: I don't want *that*, Trent. The Varros are more
than an abstraction. More than cheerful long-term care.
I want you.

TRENT: Then...please...tell me...

BOWEN: Please don't ask me. Garrett takes care of these
things—

TRENT: Garrett's not here!

BOWEN: You don't want to know.

TRENT: Yes, I do! More than anything! For Garrett's
sake—if you care about him—

BOWEN: It won't bring Garrett back! Leave it alone!

TRENT: No! I won't!

BOWEN: No good—just...more grief—

FELIX: They can't hurt you if you don't have secrets—

BOWEN: It's not my secret.

TRENT: Then tell me.

(After a moment, BOWEN *produces the cemetery rubbing.*
TRENT *stares at the rubbing a moment, then completely
breaks down, perhaps physically collapsing with a moan. The
mysterious bell tolls several times in the darkness. Lights
up to reveal* TRENT *and* FELIX *in bed, with* FELIX *holding*
TRENT *in his arms.)*

TRENT: I'm sorry.

FELIX: Shhhh.

TRENT: He didn't want you to know.

FELIX: He didn't want *you* to know.

TRENT: He's always been kind. In secret.

FELIX: Shhhh.

TRENT: I can leave tomorrow. Is that all right?

FELIX: I'd stay in New Orleans if you wanted me to.

TRENT: Nothing to stay for.

FELIX: Doesn't Bowen need—?

TRENT: He's a survivor—a female angler fish.

FELIX: If you thought he truly needed you, would you stay?

TRENT: Without question. But truth ain't his strong suit. So, regarding L A—if you still want—?

FELIX: Yes, I want. I'll take care of the tickets.

TRENT: Stubborn old bastard! Why's he make it so hard?

FELIX: Oh, my God!

TRENT: Your God what?

FELIX: I just realized why I love you.

TRENT: Why?

FELIX: Because you love *them* so much.

(*A knock at the door.* FELIX *pulls the sheet up over them more securely.*)

FELIX: Come in.

BOWEN: (*Coming in*) I'm sorry—you're not—?

FELIX: Not exactly in the mood.

BOWEN: No, of course not. (*After a moment*) They got him. Right at the Corner Pocket—dancing. Like today was any other day.

FELIX: Is he really that stupid?

BOWEN & TRENT: Yes.

(*Silence for a moment*)

TRENT: Bowen, how can I—?

BOWEN: No—quiet—

TRENT: Please—I mean—thank you. You tried—I couldn't figure out why you wouldn't tell—

BOWEN: Shhhh.

(Uncomfortable pause)

BOWEN: The...uh...young man in the attic wanted me to— *(Brandishes paper)*

TRENT: Something new?

BOWEN: Just finished. For you.

FELIX: *(Starts to get up.)* Oh, well, I can—

BOWEN: No, it's for both of you, please stay. He'd like you to.

FELIX: The young man in the attic?

BOWEN: Yes. He's dedicated it to Garrett.

(After FELIX relaxes back into TRENT's arms. BOWEN reads.)

BOWEN: I saw darkness upon the face of the waters
You gave me light
A firmament in the midst of the waters
You called it heaven
You gathered the waters together
Let the dry land appear
Let the earth bring forth grass, the herb yielding seed
The teeming, fecund earth
A miracle in the void
And finally
Man in his own image
Reflection of a god
Who didn't like the world
And so built his own

(Silence for a moment)

BOWEN: I liked our world. *(Starts to cry)*

TRENT: *(Sitting up in the bed, concerned)* Bowen—

BOWEN: And y'all are our apocalypse.

TRENT: It's my fault Garrett died—that idiot hustler followed *me* home—but I can't change that now!

BOWEN: You could stay.

TRENT: We've lost what held our world together.

BOWEN: Stay with me! I told you the truth when you demanded it! Exposed in the harshest light—

FELIX: *(Jumping out of the bed, putting his arms around* BOWEN.*)* You can always build another world.

BOWEN: *(Losing control)* Garrett—built.

FELIX: *(Guiding* BOWEN *to the bed)* He can still.

TRENT: For God's sake, Felix—

BOWEN: *(Overlapping)* Don't start with that phantom crap.

TRENT: *(Overlapping)* Enough of that new agey—shaman stuff—

FELIX: If Garrett created your world, he's gotta have that Father, Son and Holy Ghost thing going on.

BOWEN: Young man, that's just a poem.

*(*GARRETT *appears, unseen.)*

FELIX: *(Sees* GARRETT *although the others do not)* Oh, my God!

TRENT: What?

FELIX: Don't you—can't you—?

TRENT: Today's not the day for this seeing things—

FELIX: I always wanted to see—

BOWEN: *(Looking where* FELIX *is looking, not seeing* GARRETT*)* You're an odd and even eerie young person.

FELIX: —And understand—

BOWEN: Trent, you can't go to L A with him till he's had an exorcism.

FELIX: I think I understand what ghosts are.

BOWEN: I don't believe in ghosts.

TRENT: Felix, you know I don't.

FELIX: But you believe in history, don't you?

TRENT: I guess so.

BOWEN: Of course.

FELIX: And history's what holds us together.

(GARRETT *leans in to kiss* FELIX, *who hesitates a fraction of a second, then accepts the kiss.*)

TRENT: That and secrets.

FELIX: *(Gently pulling out of the kiss)* Why don't we keep those in the archive?

(FELIX *continues staring at* GARRETT.)

BOWEN: *(To* TRENT*)* Which is your responsibility now.

(BOWEN *does not notice when* GARRETT *takes his hand.* TRENT *does not notice when* GARRETT *takes his hand.*)

TRENT: Can you adapt to the light?

BOWEN: An honest attempt.

TRENT: *(After a moment)* All right.

BOWEN: Thank you, Felix.

TRENT: Felix, what are you doing?

FELIX: I'm sorry. Are...are your hands cold?

TRENT: One of them.

BOWEN: *(Rubbing one hand with the other, not knowing he's caressing* GARRETT's*)* A little.

FELIX: Then get closer. We need to keep each other warm.

TRENT: Get closer? I'm already uncomfortable.

FELIX: Sometimes warmth is.

| BOWEN; | TRENT: |
| Oh, stop. | Felix— |

FELIX: Closer.

TRENT: Ow...sorry. *(Pause)* How long do we have to sit like this?

FELIX: As long as we need to.

(FELIX starts slightly when he notices one of BOWEN's hands caressing him in a very familiar way.)

BOWEN: *(Fully recovered from his tears)* None of that goddamned sentimentality! That's why we have poems, so we have a place to put all those finer feelings that are so inconvenient and impractical in daily life—

(As BOWEN speaks, FELIX looks to TRENT, who notices BOWEN's caress of FELIX as well. TRENT just shrugs and grins sheepishly. FELIX relaxes and grins as well, accepting BOWEN's touch.)

BOWEN: Young people romanticize everything. Every song on the radio absolutely reeks of profundity—you get a lotta truly erroneous information from love songs on the radio.

(GARRETT slowly draws his hands together, binding BOWEN and TRENT tightly to FELIX.)

BOWEN: Not one about sebaceous cysts, trimming each others' ear hairs and farting in bed. Most certainly the striking difference between the old and the young. Well, that and sex. You think love will save you, when of course you have no idea in the world what love is. And don't look to your elders to tell you because we don't know either.

(They are all tightly bound together in GARRETT's *embrace, happy but unconsciously so.* GARRETT's *hand is on* BOWEN's *shoulder.)*

BOWEN: Life doesn't get any less confusing as you near the end, but you find yourself grateful for any little feeling, even a little pain. Speaking of which, move your elbow, goddammit, you're jabbing the hell outta me. Shit.

END OF PLAY